Contents

Harvest time!

Harvest is the time of year when farmers gather in all the food they have grown. People all over the world have celebrated harvest for hundreds of years.

Today, farmers harvest crops with modern machines like this combine harvester.

4

We Love
HARVEST

Honor Head

WAYLAND

First published in Great Britain in 2007 by
Wayland, an imprint of Hachette Children's Books

Reprinted in 2008

Hachette Children's Books
338 Euston Road, London NW1 3BH

Produced for Wayland by Q2A
Editor: Jean Coppendale
Senior Design Manager: Simmi Sikka
Designer: Diksha Khatri
Consultants: Maurice Lyon; Jane Clements and Rachel
Montagu from the Council of Christians and Jews

A catalogue record for this book is available from
the British Library.

ISBN 978 0 7502 5256 0

Printed in China

Wayland is a division of Hachette Children's Books,
an Hachette Livre UK company.
www.hachettelivre.co.uk

The publishers would like to thank the following for
allowing us to reproduce their pictures in this book:
AGCO Corporation: 4 / Michael Kopka: 5 / Corbis: title
page, 6, Phil Schermeister; 13, Gail Mooney; 14, David H.
Wells; 22, Caroline Penn; 23, Wolfgang Kaehler /
REUTERS: cover, 7, Vasily Fedosenko; 17, Sherwin Crasto /
Alamy: 8, archivberlin Fotoagentur GmbH / www.
photographersdirect.com: 9, Richard Levine Photography;
10, Dennis MacDonald; 18, Ashok Jain / Betty Sederquist:
11 / Photolibrary: 12, Foodpix / Leubitz: 15 / THE
HINDU: 16, 19 / David Boughey: 20 / Istockphoto: 21,
Norman Chan.

Many years ago, the only food people had to eat was the food they grew themselves. If the harvest was poor, there would not be enough food for everyone. To celebrate a good harvest, there would be a big **feast** with singing, dancing and games.

In the past, the horse and cart which brought home the last load of the harvest was decorated with flowers and ribbons.

5

Country fairs and festivals

Harvest Festival normally takes place in the **autumn,** at the time of the full or Harvest Moon. There are often fairs and festivals with stalls, rides, music and dancing in the countryside.

In Canada there are harvest fairs where people dress up to celebrate.

In many countries, music festivals and street parades are held for people to celebrate harvest time.

These girls from Belarus, near Russia, are dressed in their **national costume** for a harvest parade.

Giving thanks

Many people take part in a special **church service** at harvest time. They decorate their church and give thanks to God for a good harvest by praying and singing **hymns**.

Flowers, fresh fruit and vegetables make a colourful display in the church.

People bring gifts of food to the church. These are put on show as a reminder of the good things they believe God gives them. The food is later given to the poor.

This high school boy in the USA is serving a special harvest dinner to the elderly.

Celebrating at school

In many countries children bring tinned and fresh food to their harvest display in school.

Many schools have special Harvest Festival activities. In assembly, the children give thanks for what they have. They also think about people who are not as well off as they are.

In some countries, the last sheaf of corn of the harvest was made into a doll shape. This was to please the Corn Spirit so there would be a good harvest the next year.

In the USA, school children learn how to make corn dollies.

Thanksgiving, USA

Today at Thanksgiving families share a big roast turkey meal.

In the United States, there is a **national holiday** called Thanksgiving. It is always on the fourth Thursday in November.

Hundreds of years ago some people from England decided to settle in America. They were called the Pilgrim Fathers. They celebrated the first Thanksgiving, a special service to thank God for their first harvest.

On every Thanksgiving Day, the colourful Macy's Day Parade takes place in New York.

DID YOU KNOW?

The first harvest feast was enjoyed by the Pilgrim Fathers and the Native Americans, who helped them to settle in their new land.

Friendship and joy

The sukkah reminds families of the time the Jews lived in the wilderness.

Sukkot is the Jewish festival to thank God for the harvest. Sukkot lasts for seven or eight days. Family and friends spend time together having fun. Some families build an outdoor hut called a sukkah, where they eat and sleep.

During Sukkot, many Jews wave the Four Species. They also say a prayer to give thanks to God for the harvest and to ask for rain to bring a good harvest the next year.

This boy is holding the Four Species: a palm branch, three myrtle twigs, two willow stems and a fruit called citron.

15

Let's party

Onam is a harvest festival held in Kerala, India, in August or September. Lots of people take part in dancing and singing in the streets and let off fireworks.

Actors in costumes and masks perform in the streets during the harvest celebrations in India.

The celebrations include elephant parades, and entertainers dressed up in masks and costumes. Onam begins with the exciting Snake Boat Race. Many people decorate their boats with flowers, before they race to the beat of big drums.

These two teams are getting ready to begin the Snake Boat Race in India.

Dancing with joy

Baisakhi is the **Sikh** New Year. It is also a celebration of the harvest in a part of India called the Punjab. It takes place in April, which is when **winter-grown crops** are gathered in. Everyone wears their best clothes and there is lots of music and dancing.

Indian dancers celebrate the harvest.

As part of the celebrations many people go to their gurdwara, the Sikhs' place of worship. They give thanks for the good harvest and leave sweets or money for the poor.

In some parts of India, people begin Baisakhi by bathing in the rivers. This is to make sure they are clean before they pray to God.

Under the Moon

The Harvest Moon Festival in China takes place in mid-autumn, when the Moon is the brightest it will be all year. It is a time to celebrate a good harvest and also to meet up with old friends and family, and think about loved ones.

These Chinese children wear their best clothes for a Moon festival parade.

Many people eat special Moon cakes under the light of the full Moon. The children listen to the Story of the Moon Fairy, or Lady of the Moon, who dances on the Moon once a year. In the parks there are plays and shows to enjoy.

Moon cakes can have a sweet filling made from seasame, walnut and lotus seeds. Some are filled with ham or duck eggs.

Festival of Yams

These villagers who live on an island in the South Pacific share out the harvest of yams.

A yam is a vegetable. In many places, such as West Africa, it is one of the main foods that everyone eats. Every August the Festival of Yams celebrates the harvest of the yam crop.

Dancers wearing masks tell the story of the good ghost who protects the growing yams from the bad ghosts, so that people have plenty of yams to eat.

Masked dancers ask God for a good crop of yams next year.

DID YOU KNOW?

In parts of Africa, twins and triplets are thought to be a gift from God. They are given special treatment during the Yam festival.

Index and glossary

autumn the season between summer and winter

church service when people gather at certain times in church to pray to God, sing hymns and listen to readings from the Bible

feast a big meal with lots of special food shared with friends

hymns religious songs of praise that are sung in church

national costume special clothes worn only by people from a certain country

national holiday a time when no one goes to school or work

Sikhs people who believe in a religion called Sikhism

triplets the name for three babies born at the same time to the same mother

winter-grown crop food which is grown during the winter months